Prehistoric North America

# When Life Flourished in Ancient Seas

## The Early Paleozoic Era

*Jean F. Blashfield with Richard P. Jacobs*

Customer Service 888-454-2279
Visit our website at www.heinemannlibrary.com

**Produced for Heinemann Library by Books Two, Inc.**
Editorial: Jean Black, Deborah Grahame
Design: Michelle Lisseter
Illustrations: John T. Wallace, Top-Notch Productions
Picture Research: JLM Visuals
Production: Jean Black

Originated by Modern Age Repro
Printed and bound by South China Printing Company

10 09 08 07 06
10 9 8 7 6 5 4 3 2 1

**Library of Congress Cataloging-in-Publication Data**
Blashfield, Jean F.
  When life flourished in ancient seas : the paleozoic era / Jean F. Blashfield and Richard P. Jacobs.
     p. cm. -- (Prehistoric North America)
  Includes bibliographical references and index.
  ISBN 1-4034-7658-6
  1. Earth--Juvenile literature. I. Jacobs, Richard P. II. Title. III. Series: Blashfield, Jean F. Prehistoric North America.
  QB631.4.B58 2005
  560′.172--dc22

                         2004027400

Geology consultant: Marli Bryant Miller, Ph.D., University of Oregon
Maps: Ronald C, Blakey, Ph.D., Northern Arizona University
PICTURE CREDITS: COVER: Underwater Reef, Dr. James P. McVey, NOAA Sea Grant Program; Ammonite, Breck P. Kent.TITLE PAGE: Coral reef, Marli Miller
INTERIOR: Balkwell, David: 72 Archean; Blegen, Don: 60 bot; Crangle, Charlie: 73 Jurassic; The Field Museum: 18, 58, 66, 68, 71, 72 Cambrian, Silurian, Permian, 73 Paleocene, Miocene, Pliocene; Gernant, Robert: 11 top; Gilbert, Gordon R.: 73 Eocene; Greenler, Robert: 62 top; Harms, Carl: 2; Jacobs, Richard P.: Page borders, 7, 8, 10 top, 10 bot left, 11 top right, 11 bot left, 11 bot right, 12, 23 top, 23 center, 29, 31, 33 left, 34, 35 top, 39 bot, 40, 44, 47 bot, 45 bot, 46 top, 52 top, 52 bot, 55 top, 56 bot, 57 top right, 57 bot right, 59, 60 top, 69 top, 69 bot; Kent, Breck P.: 2, 10 top left, 10 bot right, 22, 23 bot, 32 bot, 33 right, 45 top, 46 bot, 47 top, 53 top, 53 bot left, 53 bot right, 55 bot, 56 top, 57 bot left, 64 top, 72 Ordovician, Devonian, Mississippian, 73 Holocene; Kerstitch, Alex: 58 bot; Larson, Alden C.: 48; Laudon, Lowell R.: 13 top, 20 top; Leszczynski, Zig: 73 Oligocene; Miller, Marli: 4, 9, 13 bot, 35 bot, 36, 39 top, 42, 43, 62 bot, 73 Pleistocene; Minnich, John: 41; NOAA: 26, 53 bot center, 64 bot; NPS: 24; Smith, David A.: 54; Smithsonian National Museum of Natural History: 16, 20 bot, 63, 70, 72 Proterozoic, Pennsylvanian; Snead, Rodman E.: 32 top, 61 top, 65; USDA/ARS: 61 bot; USDA/NRCS: 28; University of Michigan Exhibit Museum: 50, 57 top, 67 top, 67 bot, 73 Triassic.

Some words are shown in bold, **like this**. You can find the definitions for these words in the glossary.

# Contents

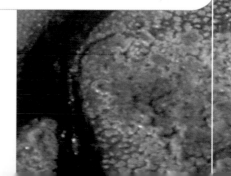

# Chapter 1

# The Scene as the Paleozoic Started

The time period in Earth history called the Paleozoic Era began about 543 million years ago. Earth had been in existence for more than 4 billion years before the Paleozoic. During these 4 billion years, an amazing number of events happened on the third planet from the sun. These events would make Earth different from every other planet in the solar system.

The rock that formed the planet became hot. It gradually melted into a partially liquid form called **magma**. This material contained all of the natural chemical elements that Earth would ever have. Over time, the magma separated into layers. Heavy metals, especially iron and nickel, sank to the center. This formed a metal **core**. The center of the core is solid and the outer half is melted to a liquid state, or **molten**.

The huge upper layer of Earth is called the **mantle**. It is a mixture of rock and crystallized minerals. The mantle contains a great deal of iron and magnesium. The mantle's materials are hard, but they can still flow over long periods of time.

Rock on the surface of the mantle formed a **crust**. The crust and the upper part of the mantle are called the **lithosphere**. The **asthenosphere** lies beneath the lithosphere. This is the hotter, more fluid part of the earth's mantle. The crust was on the move. It "floated" around on the surface of the planet. Sometimes huge chunks of the crust clustered together. These chunks formed a **supercontinent**. At other times, the supercontinent broke apart. This took place during the final hundreds of millions of years before the Paleozoic Era started.

↰ *Hot lava pouring through Earth's crust becomes rock that makes new land.*

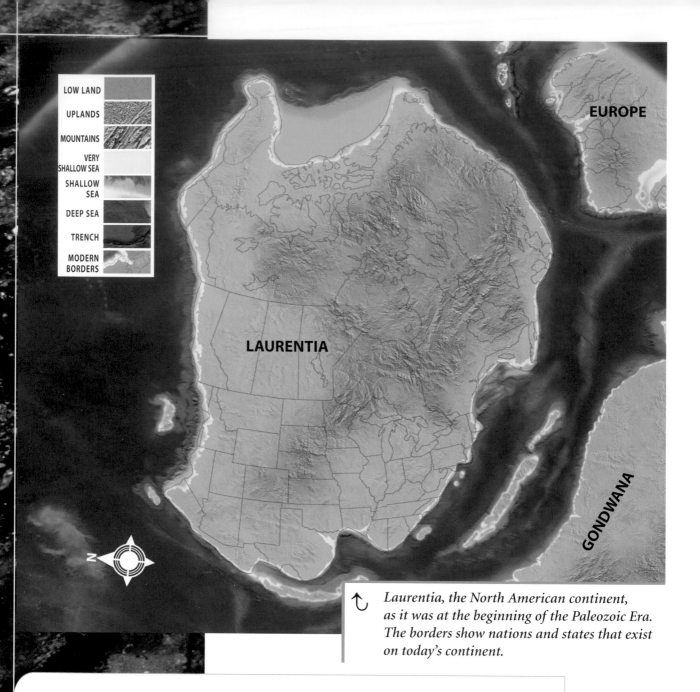

### Legend

- LOW LAND
- UPLANDS
- MOUNTAINS
- VERY SHALLOW SEA
- SHALLOW SEA
- DEEP SEA
- TRENCH
- MODERN BORDERS

EUROPE

LAURENTIA

GONDWANA

N

*Laurentia, the North American continent, as it was at the beginning of the Paleozoic Era. The borders show nations and states that exist on today's continent.*

Some bits of crust gathered to form a smaller continent. Scientists call that early continent **Laurentia**, after the Laurentian Mountains of Canada. Laurentia became a **craton**, or stable (unchanging) rock core of a continent. North America would be built on this craton.

An atmosphere formed around the planet, too. At first, it consisted of poisonous gases. These gases rose out of the mantle. But mixed in with the poisonous gases was water vapor. Soon this water vapor condensed as drops, which fell as rain onto the rapidly cooling planet. Enough water eventually fell to form an ocean that covered most of the planet.

After perhaps half a billion years, microscopic living things began to grow in the ocean. These living things were a special kind of **bacteria** that gave off oxygen. The oxygen rose from the sea into the atmosphere. Earth was changing into a place that could support life of many different kinds.

## Looking at Fossils

We know about ancient living things by the remains they left behind—their **fossils**. The word *fossil* means "dug up." Since ancient Greek times, people have been interested in the rocky remains of animals they dug up. However, until recently, they could not explain where the fossils came from. People assumed that all **species**, or kinds of plants and animals, came into existence at one time. They believed these species all still existed.

In the 1700s, the new field of geology fascinated many people who were interested in the natural world. Some of these naturalists concentrated on the field of **paleontology**. They found fossils of some animals that did not resemble anything living. Other scientists believed that living examples of these fossils would still be found.

*Early naturalists were mystified by the fossils they found in rocks.*

## Ahead of His Time

One of the first people to recognize that fossils were remains of ancient life was the artist and inventor Leonardo da Vinci (1452–1519). Some people of his time thought that marine fossils found in the Apennine Mountains of Italy had been washed there by the 40-day flood of Noah's time. But Leonardo doubted that was the answer. He recorded his idea in his notebooks. Da Vinci suggested that the fossil-filled land had once been a low seacoast before being raised up as mountains.

*Fossils of mastodons were among the evidence 19th-century scientists used to show that some living things had become extinct in the past.*

French paleontologist Georges Cuvier disagreed with this position. He demonstrated that various species had become **extinct** in the past. Cuvier did this by using fossils found in the Paris area. Fossils of mammoths, ancient relatives of elephants, for example, had been found in the 1700s.

Cuvier was certain that living specimens of these elephant ancestors were not going to be found by explorers. And pioneers in America had found fossils of

# Georges Cuvier, Founder of Paleontology

Cuvier (1769–1832) was born in the Jura Mountains section of France. He became a tutor and local government official. These jobs gave him plenty of time to explore his first love, the natural world. He became famous as a scholar of biology. He was only 26 when he was called to work at the new National Museum of Natural History in Paris. Cuvier's work on fossils and the extinction of living things inspired the scientific community. It led to serious exploration into the idea that Earth is much older than people had thought. Cuvier wrote, "Why has not anyone seen that fossils alone gave birth to a theory about the formation of the earth, that without them, no one would have ever dreamed that there were successive epochs in the formation of the globe." Cuvier's study of living and fossil animals demonstrated these new ideas clearly. Indeed, there have been animals that existed in the past that did not exist anymore. With this study, he began the modern science of paleontology.

mastodons, which are also elephant relatives. They did not find any specimens, however. Clearly, both mammoths and mastodons—quite different from today's elephants in Asia and Africa— had become extinct. In 1796, Cuvier presented a paper on the subject of extinction of species. No one had the facts to prove him wrong.

## Fossil Basics

Not every animal or plant forms a fossil. In fact, very few do. When most living things die, their bodies decay, or rot, on the ground or under water. Conditions have to be exactly right for a fossil to form. The living things themselves have to have parts that might fossilize.

The earliest forms of life were single-celled creatures. Bacteria are single-celled creatures in existence today. They first appeared during the long stretch of time called the Precambrian. They were the only life on Earth for billions of years. Traces of these one-celled creatures rarely survived the upheavals of the young Earth. Animals gradually became larger and developed hard shells or, later, skeletons. Fossils then formed in greater numbers. This was during the

*The long lumps on this rock are **trace fossils** that may be fossilized burrows of wormlike animals.*

beginning of the time covered by this book, the first half of the Paleozoic **Era**. *Paleozoic* means "ancient life."

During the early part of the Paleozoic Era, many animals evolved that had hard parts, such as shells and even skeletons. But it wasn't usually the shell or bone itself that became a fossil. Instead, the object fell to the bottom of a body of water. There it became part of the **scdiment**, such as sand, dirt, and debris. Chemicals in water gradually changed the object. The chemicals replaced the materials that made up the shell of the dead animal, atom for atom.

# Examining Kinds of Fossilization

These fossils represent various ways that fossils are formed. The actual remains of ancient life are rare.

This large collection of bones was found preserved in the La Brea Tar Pits of southern California. Many now-extinct animals fell into the tar. Parts of their bodies were preserved.

This insect fossil is the actual remains of an ancient insect. It was trapped in the tree resin (like sap). The resin later hardened into **amber**. Such preservation is one type of fossil.

Replacement is another, more common type of fossilization. The original living material is replaced by minerals dissolved in underground water. **Silica** replaced the original material of this **brachiopod** (left). The original material of the **ammonite** (right) was largely replaced by the mineral **pyrite**.

**Petrified wood** formed when the original tissue of the tree was replaced by silica, cell by cell. Silica also filled pores in the wood. Petrified means "turned to stone." The exact original structure of the tree, including growth rings, was duplicated by the silica.

Perhaps only a single leaf of a tree or plant was preserved, instead. Just a thin film of the element carbon in the shape of a delicate fern leaf might remain. This form of fossilization is called carbonized impression.

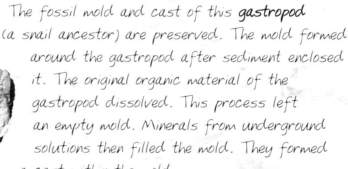

The fossil mold and cast of this **gastropod** (a snail ancestor) are preserved. The mold formed around the gastropod after sediment enclosed it. The original organic material of the gastropod dissolved. This process left an empty mold. Minerals from underground solutions then filled the mold. They formed a cast within the mold made by the gastropod.

This footprint was made by a dinosaur. It is not the actual remains or the replaced remains of the dinosaur. The footprint gives evidence of ancient life, however. This kind of evidence is called a trace fossil.

An object that has fossilized in sediment may be dug up millions of years later. It would then appear to be identical to the animal that had been buried. The main chemicals that form such fossils are **carbonates** (carbon-oxygen combinations) and silica (silicon-oxygen combinations).

Plant fossils are often found as mere **carbon** traces, especially in the layers of rock called **shale**. A branch of a plant might fall into sediment. It remains there as the sediment turns to rock. Most parts of the plant dissolve away. Only the carbon remains to leave a "print" of the branch. Coal is made from the carbon in plants. It is often called a fossil fuel.

↩ *Algae* *became fossilized more easily than land plants.* *This is because seawater prevented plant matter from* *rotting before it fossilized.*

# Index Fossils

In the late 18th century, a surveyor named William Smith (1769–1839) worked on planning a canal system for England. He identified layers of rock in different locations. He noticed that different kinds of fossils appeared in the same order. This was the case no matter what kind of rock they were in. He realized he could use fossils to describe rock order. His work was so accurate that he drew up the first geological map of England.

At the same time, across the English Channel, Georges Cuvier was studying the fossils around Paris. He saw that no matter which rock beds he was studying, the fossils he found were in the same order.

*This red **sandstone** shows clearly how **sedimentary rock** is deposited in layers. The differences in the layers are made by changes in sediment, climate, ocean depth, and the kinds of minerals in the water.* ↰

He began to use certain fossils as indicators of the **relative age** (which came first or second) of various rocks. Such fossils are called **index fossils**. Together, Smith and Cuvier started stratigraphy, the science of using rock layers and the fossils found in them to establish earth history.

Stratigraphers search for fossils of species that lived in a wide variety of areas. These species must also have lived during narrow and specific periods of time. Thus if the fossil is found, geologists know that the rock was laid down during a fairly specific time period.

*The small shells of* Lingula *brachiopods are found in so much rock from so many time periods that they are not useful as index fossils.* ↰

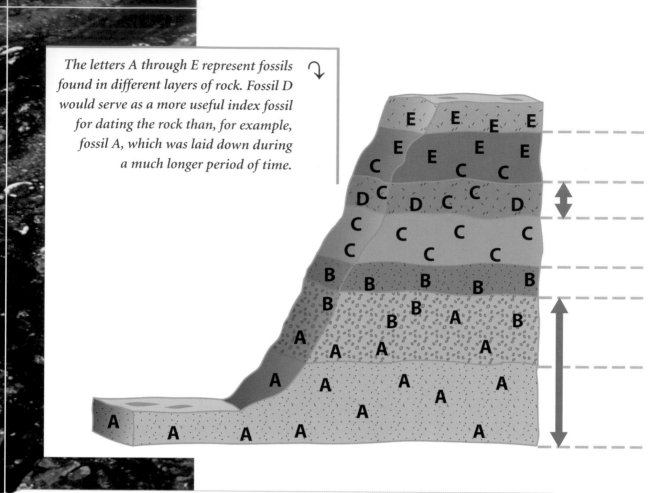

*The letters A through E represent fossils found in different layers of rock. Fossil D would serve as a more useful index fossil for dating the rock than, for example, fossil A, which was laid down during a much longer period of time.*

If a species existed for a long period of time, it would not be possible to narrow down the time period when the rock was formed. For example, the *Lingula* is found in rocks dating from half a billion years ago. This burrowing, shelled animal is still found today. Its appearance in rock indicates almost nothing about the age of the rock.

## Geologic Time

Geologists of the 18th and 19th centuries worked on developing a time line that would show the history of life on Earth. They realized that such a time line would be more accurate if it were based on fossils instead of on the rocks themselves. Two different locations might have quite different kinds of rocks. If they contained the same index fossils, then the rocks were the same age.

A paleontologist carefully removes the →
rock around fossilized dinosaur bones.
Dinosaur bones are found only in rock that
was deposited during the Mesozoic Era.

Naturalists noticed something interesting about the many fossils of shelled animals in the rocks they were studying. The fossils seemed to appear all at once. Naturalists thought that life began that way, suddenly and with a great flourish, about 600 million years ago.

They called the time when these shelled animals appeared the Cambrian. It was named for rocks they studied in Wales. Cambria was the ancient name for Wales. Anything that happened before the appearance of the shelled animals was called *Pre*cambrian. The Precambrian makes up most of Earth's history—a full 88 percent.

Paleontologists studied rocks around the world. They analyzed layer upon layer of rock. They divided geologic time after the Precambrian into three huge eras. They based these divisions on when there were major changes in the kinds of fossils being found.

*Paleontologists at science and natural history museums create scenes of what life was probably like long ago. They base the scenes on the fossils discovered from specific time periods. This is a scene of marine life during the Silurian Period, about 430 million years ago. A large **trilobite** (left) and a **cephalopod** (right) are feeding on a coral **reef**. Smaller trilobites are on the sand nearby.*

First was the Paleozoic Era, meaning "ancient life." It started with the great sudden appearance of shelled animals. It ended when most of them disappeared. The Mesozoic Era, for "middle life," ended when there was another great disappearance, including dinosaurs. Finally, there was the Cenozoic Era, meaning "recent life." We are still in the Cenozoic Era today. These three eras make up Phanerozoic time, meaning "revealed life."

The entire **geologic time scale** is found on pages 72 and 73. This book concerns the first part of the Paleozoic Era. It covers from the start of the Cambrian 543 million years ago to the end of the Devonian Period, 354 million years ago.

By 1900, geologists and paleontologists had generally agreed on a geologic time scale. But what they agreed on was relative time, not

**absolute time**. In other words, they agreed on the order in which things occurred on Earth but not on exactly when the events happened.

Scientists could not measure absolute time at first. They had to discover that certain chemical elements change over time at a very specific rate. Dates in the geologic time scale are subject to change. This is because geologists continue to find more ancient rocks and to establish dates for them.

**PRECAMBRIAN TIME** • *4.5 billion to 543 million years ago*

**PALEOZOIC ERA** • *543 to 248 million year ago*

| Time Period | Tectonic Events | Biological Events |
|---|---|---|
| **Cambrian Period** *543–248 million years ago* Named for old name of Wales | Laurentia separated from Siberia | Cambrian Explosion: Major diversification of marine invertebrates |
| **Ordovician Period** *490–443 million years ago* Named for a Celtic tribe in Wales | First Iapetus Ocean Taconic orogeny in northeastern Laurentia | First true vertebrates: jawless fish First land plants Mass extinction |
| **Silurian Period** *443–417 million years ago* Named for a Celtic tribe in Wales | Caledonian orogeny Shallow seas on Laurentia | First vascular plants First insects First jawed fish |
| **Devonian Period** *417–354 million years ago* Named for Devon, England | Major reef building | First forests First seed–baring plants First four–footed animals First amphibians |
| **Mississippian Epoch** *354–323 million years ago* Named for Mississippi River Valley | Antler orogeny | Ferns abundant First land vertebrates |
| **Pennsylvanian Epoch** *323–290 million years ago* Named for coal formations in Pennsylvania | Appalachian orogeny began | Ferns abundant Major coal–forming forests First reptiles |
| **Permian** *290–248 million years ago* Named for Russian province of Perm | Pangea formed | First warm–blooded reptiles Greatest mass extinction |

*PHANEROZOIC TIME • 543 million years ago to present*

*PALEOZOIC ERA • 543 to 248 million years ago*

*CARBONIFEROUS PERIOD 354 to 290 million years ago*

**MESOZOIC ERA** • *248 to 65 million years ago*
**CENOZOIC ERA** • *65 million years ago to present*

# Chapter 2

# The Cambrian Explosion

Early paleontologists recognized that new kinds of living things appeared suddenly at the start of the Cambrian. The rocks and fossils from this period date back to more than half a billion years ago. They show an astonishing variety and experimentation in the **evolution** of animals. Some new species succeeded. Others gradually disappeared. Within a period of not more than a few million years every **phylum** (major group of animals or plants) known today appeared.

# Fossil Motherlodes

Most of what we know about Cambrian marine animal life comes from a few sources. These sources are called "motherlodes." This means that they are the main source of information. There are three known motherlodes of Cambrian fossils. Two are in North America and one is in China. In each case, remains of soft-bodied animals are found in shale rock.

The oldest motherlode is located in northern Greenland. It was discovered in 1984 on the eastern shore of a **fjord**, by A.K. Higgins of the Geological Survey of Greenland. He named the heavily fossiled site Sirius Passet after a sled patrol that worked in the area. Scientists have dug up at least 10,000 specimens at Sirius Passet.

The Burgess Shale was the first motherlode discovered. It was found in 1909. The fossil-containing rock was laid down during the Middle Cambrian, about 505 million years ago. Burgess Shale is an area on a ridge between two mountains in Yoho National Park in British Columbia near Mount Burgess.

This motherlode was an important first discovery. It confirmed the great explosion of life that took place at the beginning of the Paleozoic Era. The Burgess Shale preserved fossils of animals that lived in a warm shallow sea. They were apparently swamped by a mudslide. As a result, they were buried instantly on the seafloor.

The third motherlode was found in 1985 in **mudstones** of Chengjiang, China. These mudstones date from the same period as the Burgess Shale.

↰ *A museum display of a marine environment during the Cambrian Period*

# The Burgess Shale

Some of the finest fossils in the world are found in the Burgess Shale near Field, British Columbia. This shale is rich in fossils. It is found at the higher elevations of the Canadian Rockies, along the Continental Divide. The Burgess Shale is dark, almost black in color. It was formed during the Cambrian in a marine environment.

Many of the fossils found in the shale are trilobites. These were crablike, shelled animals or their close relatives. They were usually between 1 and 4 inches (2.5 to 10 cm) long. The shale also contains sponges, worms, jellyfish, and other soft-bodied animals. Extremely delicate parts of these animals are seen preserved in the shale as carbonized impressions.

Good fossils of such soft-bodied animals and their delicate parts are extremely rare. Those in the Burgess Shale were preserved in a fascinating process. The animals were quickly buried in sediment and in water containing little oxygen. When this happened the bodies of the buried soft-bodied animals were protected from scavengers and rapid decay.

When the Burgess Shale was developing, the area was on the western edge of Laurentia, which was located on the equator. Millions of years later, that part of the seafloor was raised as mountains. Huge **faults** or cracks broke apart the rock. The land containing the fossils was moved eastward and thousands of feet upward. This was where the fossils were found in the 20th century. Digging in the region is still going on. Fossil beds have also been found in neighboring Kootenay National Park.

# Trilobites

**Arthropods** are animals that have an outer shell, or exoskeleton, in segments, or sections, and many legs. Today, spiders, insects, and lobsters are common arthropods. They made their first appearance during the early Paleozoic. In fact, it was the sudden widespread appearance of one group of arthropods, the trilobites, that originally determined the break between Precambrian and Cambrian times.

## HOW DO THEY KNOW
## Where to Start the Cambrian?

They don't! If you were to look in an older geology book, you would find the Paleozoic Era labeled as beginning about 600 million years ago. For a century, geologists were fairly sure they knew when Precambrian times ended and Paleozoic times began. They established a boundary that depended on a tiny creature called a trilobite. The boundary was set at the time when these index fossils first appeared.

In the 1970s, however, paleontologists found more primitive shelled animals. They were found in layers of rock beneath the trilobite fossils. These fossils were much smaller than trilobites. They represented many different large groups, or phyla, of animals. The fossils included sponges, mollusks, and worms. The paleontologists officially called these primitive creatures "small shelly fossils."

In the late 1990s, geologists found that living things bigger than microscopic beings may have existed as early as 670 million years ago. Finally, the scientists decided that there was not a clear break between the Precambrian and the Cambrian. They agreed to use 543 million years ago as the boundary between the periods of time just for convenience. However, they might change the date again as new discoveries are made.

Trilobites had three visible sections (*tri-* means "three") running backward from the head. That characteristic makes them easy to identify in rocks. Trilobite fossils were important markers. They confirmed that continents have moved throughout history. Paleontologists found that some rocks in Newfoundland contained the same trilobite fossils as a region of northern Wales, 1,365 miles (2,200 km) away. During the Cambrian, these two regions were attached to each other.

Trilobites were among the most abundant and diverse animals of the Cambrian Period. They also lived during the remainder of the Paleozoic Era. They became extinct at the end of that era. This is a well-defined time period. As a result, trilobites are useful index fossils for identifying Paleozoic rock. Almost half of Paleozoic fossil types are trilobites.

The marine environment of the evolving Paleozoic animals was not the deep ocean. Instead, they evolved in warm shallow seas. These seas covered most of what was then Laurentia. Sunlight can penetrate and warm the water in such shallow seas. Microscopic plants easily grow in these conditions. There was plenty of food to support evolving animal life.

It was not only life that was changing during the early Paleozoic Era. The future North America itself was growing and changing.

## A Giant of a Trilobite

There were many different species of trilobites during the Paleozoic. These shelly animals were usually small. But in 2000, Canadian researchers working near Manitoba found the damaged shell of a trilobite. It was more than twice as large as any found before. This trilobite was almost 30 inches (75 cm) long. The discovery was a surprise to zoologists. They had been certain that marine animals of tropical waters (where Laurentia was at the time) were all fairly small. They believed that larger animals could live only in colder waters.

# Examining Trilobites

The bodies of all trilobites were divided into three segments, or lobes. The **exoskeletons** of these arthropods were strengthened with the mineral calcium carbonate, or **calcite**. This hard exoskeleton was molted, or shed, when the animal was growing. The animal's body secreted a new exoskeleton when a growth spurt was over. These exoskeletons were found fossilized.

Many trilobite fossils show that the animals had highly developed eyes. Some trilobites had eyes on the end of stalk-like appendages. And some trilobites seem to have had no eyes at all. Various gradual changes in the species, or adaptations, give scientists more information. These changes show that most of these arthropods were scavengers that crawled and fed along the bottom of ancient seas.

This coiled trilobite lived during the Devonian, at the end of which these primitive animals became extinct.

# Chapter 3

# The Changing Face of Laurentia

North America at the beginning of the Paleozoic Era did not look much like the continent today. It had quite a different shape. It was completely barren, just empty rock projecting from the ocean. There was as yet no life that could live on land. Also, the young continent was located along the equator. What would later become Canada faced east instead of north. But fossils and sediments began to play a very important role. They helped to turn Laurentia into the more recognizable continent of North America.

During the 4 billion years before the Paleozoic, the basic, stable heart of Laurentia had been formed from Earth's crust. Large chunks of crust, formed at various times, gathered, collided, separated, and finally stuck together. This formed the continent's craton. Over the eons, the craton was covered by newer sedimentary rock, and much of the craton is still covered. However, when the **glaciers** of the Ice Age moved across the land, they scraped off part of the sedimentary rock that had collected on the craton. The exposed portion of the craton is called the **Canadian Shield**.

When the Paleozoic started, what would become the western edge of the continent ended at about where the border between Utah and Nevada is today. But sediment had eroded from the interior of the craton. It was piling up in the ocean beyond the craton. Eventually, this sediment would turn into rock that was **uplifted** as mountains. It would become the first version of mountains that would some day become the Rockies.

The land from southern California all the way to Alaska and part of the nearby Northwest Territories was missing. Also missing were Mexico and Central America, and part of Texas. The whole of the future east coast had not yet formed either. This included Florida all the way north through the Gulf of St. Lawrence to Newfoundland. Much of this future land was still far away from Laurentia. It would be part of a southern supercontinent called Gondwana for millions of years to come.

↰ *The crust that made up the Blue Ridge Mountains collected on the eastern shore of Laurentia. Throughout this book, directions concerning Laurentia refer to today's directions even though the craton lay on its side during the Paleozoic.*

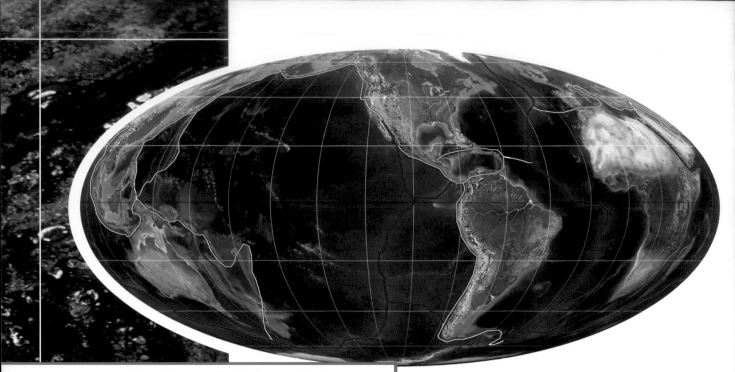

*On this map of today's **tectonic plates**, **ocean ridges**, where new crust forms, show as red lines. Yellow lines show where old crust is pulled back into the mantle.* ↰

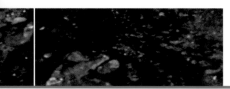

*Lava forms at spreading ridges, becoming oceanic crust. The feathery animal shown here is a feather star, a descendant of the **crinoids** that evolved during Paleozoic times.* ↱

# Moving Crust

The Paleozoic Era was a time when considerable new crust was being added to the coasts of Laurentia. By the end of the era, Laurentia would look more like the North America we recognize today. Most of this new continental land developed on the east coast. The land that was added to the continent resulted from a mountain-building episode. Such an episode is called an **orogeny**.

The landmasses of Earth had been on the move since Earth's crust had begun to form. The entire surface of the planet is divided into twelve large and several smaller segments called tectonic plates. These plates slowly move as a result of two kinds of activity that involve Earth's mantle. These activities happen at several places over the planet's surface.

The first activity is the formation of new crust under the ocean. This happens as magma oozes out through an earth-circling ocean ridge. This long ridge separates Earth's major tectonic plates. Plates that meet at these ridges are pushed apart as great quantities of new volcanic rock form. This rock forms as magma hardens. Any continents riding on these plates are also pushed apart. This process is called **seafloor spreading**.

New crust cannot continually be built without Earth getting bigger—but this doesn't happen. So the second activity comes into play. This second activity is the disappearance of oceanic crust back into the asthenosphere, which is the upper part of the mantle. This happens at trenches in the ocean floor called **subduction** zones. The crust is subducted, or drawn back, into the mantle. The moving and jerking of rock that occur during subduction are felt as earthquakes. Also, rock that melts in the heat from the mantle may rise upward through the crust. This melted rock forms volcanoes. Such volcanoes may form in the ocean or on land.

*Oceanic crust is formed and pushed apart at ocean ridges. It is subducted back into the mantle at trenches.*

These tectonic forces create oceanic crust and then cause it to disappear. These events have been going on at least since the middle of the Precambrian, about 2.5 billion years ago. By that time, most of Earth's crust had been formed. The plates continued to move around with no set pattern. Ridges and trenches formed and disappeared and reformed again.

## Growing Continents

For the first 75 million years of the Paleozoic Era, Laurentia was a fairly calm place. The only thing happening at the margins of the continent was the accumulation of thick layers of sediment. This occurred as the rocks of the craton were eroded by wind or rain. Most of the rest of Earth's crust was still a part of the huge southern supercontinent of **Gondwana**.

Then, during the Ordovician Period, about 490 million years ago, other chunks of crust began to collide with Laurentia's craton. These collisions were slow, but they occurred on a grand scale, and they formed new continental crust. The chunks of crust were carried on a tectonic plate that was subducting under the continent.

↰ *One of the primary builders of rock is sediment—sand, clay particles, and debris from living things. Even today, sediment is carried by rivers to low points, where it accumulates, as in this lake. During the early Paleozoic, such sediment accumulated along the eastern coast of Laurentia.*

Collisions at continental edges uplifted masses of rock into mountains. Sometimes this rock was sedimentary rock. This rock had formed at the edge of the continent under the sea. This is one reason fossils of marine life may be found on some mountaintops. At other times, the uplifted rock was old oceanic crust. This crust had been pushed toward Laurentia by seafloor spreading.

*Fossil brachiopods, small mollusks that* ↑
*lived in shallow marine environments*

What caused the change in Laurentia about 490 million years ago? An ancient body of water called the Iapetus Ocean lay between Laurentia and Gondwana. A new subduction zone formed on the floor of that ocean. As oceanic crust was subducted, the Iapetus Ocean shrank. A small tectonic plate bore a chunk of volcanic crust called an **island arc**. The plate was subducted, but the land on it was not dense enough to be subducted. Instead, it collided with the coast of Laurentia, where it stuck. The island arc **accreted** to the continent.

The face of Laurentia changed. This happened as the deep layers of sedimentary rock along its eastern coast were compressed. These layers were thrust upward, forming mountains.

↺ *New land can be formed as an island arc, in which volcanoes form as a result of subduction.*

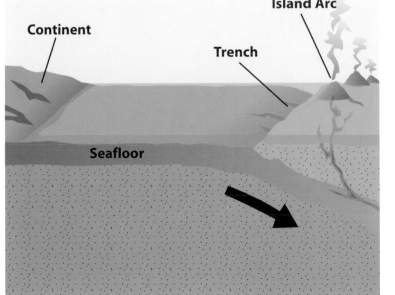

Continent

Trench

Island Arc

Seafloor

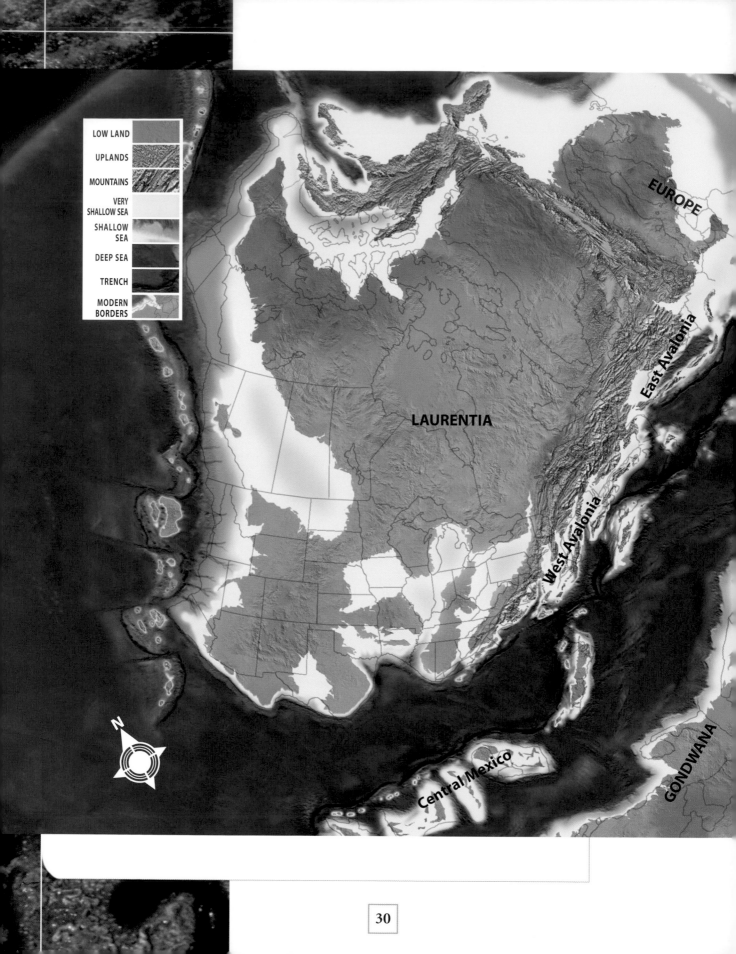

LOW LAND
UPLANDS
MOUNTAINS
VERY
SHALLOW SEA
SHALLOW
SEA
DEEP SEA
TRENCH
MODERN
BORDERS

EUROPE

East Avalonia

LAURENTIA

West Avalonia

N

Central Mexico

GONDWANA

*A series of orogenies took place during the early Paleozoic. This map shows the mountains that were pushed up by the middle of the Devonian Period along what would become the northern and eastern coasts of the North American plate. As the compass shows, the continent was no longer lying on its side. Today's northern side is nearing north. Compare the earlier map on page 38.*

Volcanoes erupted, spreading vast layers of lava (a type of **igneous rock**) throughout what is now the upper Appalachian region, from Delaware to Quebec. The heat of the collision remade the sedimentary rock into other forms called **metamorphic rock** (*metamorphosis* means "change").

This mountain-building episode is called the Taconic orogeny after the Taconic Mountains in New York State. The Taconic Mountains were built during this Ordovician orogeny. They are now almost eroded away into a plateau. The highest point is only 3,816 feet (1,163 m) above sea level.

After the Taconic orogeny calmed down, the eastern part of the continent was not left alone to erode. The Taconic was just the first episode in several collisions of large chunks of crust that would gradually create the entire Appalachian mountain system— from Alabama to Newfoundland. These later collisions happened mainly between 400 and 300 million years ago. This was when North America and some other continental cratons clustered together into the last supercontinent that formed on Earth.

*Marble is a metamorphic rock formed when heat and pressure of an orogeny changed limestone.*

During the Ordovician and Silurian periods, Laurentia was alone. It lay along the equator. Then a continent called Baltica collided with Greenland. Baltica would someday be the northwestern part of Europe. The two plates bearing Baltica and Laurentia collided with each other from north to south. This ongoing collision began when Greenland met Scandinavia. This occurred during the mountain-building period called the Caledonian. *Caledonia* is the old Latin name for Scotland.

As the two plates crashed together, odd bits of of lithosphere—called **exotic terranes**—were caught between them and became part of North America. The Avalon **terrane** was named for the Avalon Peninsula in Newfoundland. It had been part of Gondwana. After it broke away from that southern supercontinent, it somehow got caught up in the collision between Laurentia and Baltica.

## New York City's Bedrock

The base rock of the island of Manhattan in New York City was laid down in Precambrian times. Above that layer, however, is the rock that makes skyscrapers possible. This rock is called Manhattan schist. It was laid down during Ordovician times as part of the Taconic orogeny. This rock provides a solid base that can withstand the pressure exerted by the great weight of tall buildings. Schist is a type of metamorphic rock that folds in thin layers. It is visible in New York's Central Park as rock outcroppings, or exposed layers of rock.

*A New England **granite** quarry, from which*
*building stone is taken. Granite is one*
*of the primary rocks of the landscape, as above.*

Part of the Avalon terrane later broke away from Laurentia again. The part left behind became eastern New Brunswick, southeastern Nova Scotia, and New England. The Avalon terrane is noted for its granite. This gave New Hampshire the nickname of "The Granite State."

The Laurentia and Baltica plates continued to turn into each other from north to south. Another terrane shed by Gondwana got caught up. This was called the Carolina terrane. It now lies beneath the Blue Ridge Mountains, including part of North and South Carolina.

The mountains created by the Caledonian orogeny did not last long. They had eroded away by the end of the Devonian, 354 million years ago. There were rivers across most of the continent. These carried away the eroded material, along with material from the earlier Appalachians. The eroded material became the main ingredient in the continent's sedimentary rocks for most of the next 300 million years.

It was mostly quiet during the early Paleozoic. Then, a subduction zone formed along the west coast of Laurentia. Crust collected in an island arc called Antler arc. This attached itself along the whole western length of Laurentia. This attachment, or accretion, of new crust was the first of many. These would eventually make up western North America during the Mesozoic and Cenozoic eras.

## HOW DO THEY KNOW...
### The Widespread Sediment Came from the Caledonian Orogeny?

In the late 1990s, a group of geologists spread throughout North America from Texas to northern Canada. They examined the sedimentary rock called shale. They dated the samples with radioactive isotopes. They then analyzed the content. Their results showed that all the shale specimens came from the same mountain source. The eroded material had been deposited where the scientists found it. It had been deposited over a period lasting from 450 million years ago to 150 million years ago. All sediments before that time were regional. This means they had traveled only short distances before settling.

Farther north on the continent, additional mountains were starting to be built. This mountain-building event occurred along northern Canada during the late Devonian. It was called the Ellesmere orogeny. This orogeny probably resulted from contact with a section of Asian crust.

## Evaporated Minerals

Laurentia was flooded by shallow seas several times during the Paleozoic. Low areas called **basins** were often cut off from the ocean. The seawater in the basins eventually evaporated. This left behind in the basins a deposit of crystallized minerals. Over millions of years, the seas rose and fell again.

Seawater was again deposited in the basins. As the new batches of seawater evaporated, the basin deposits became thicker and thicker. The deposits gradually formed rock referred to as **evaporite**. The two most familiar evaporites are rock salt, also called **halite** (sodium chloride), and **gypsum** (calcium sulfate), which is used in making plaster and drywall.

One basin covered 170,000 square miles (440,000 sq km). It was located under what are now Michigan, Ontario, Ohio, Pennsylvania, New York, and West Virginia. This basin contains a layer 2,300 feet (700 m) thick. It has alternating levels of salt, shale, and limestone. There is a huge bed of rock salt below the city of Detroit. It lies almost 1,200 feet (366 m) below the city. The bed was mined for almost a century. The creation of this salt ended about 390 million years ago, during the Devonian.

*Halite is the mineral sodium chloride, also called rock salt and table salt. It can occur in huge deposits left by ancient evaporated seas.*

*Gypsum is the mineral calcium sulfate, seen here in a thin vein in the soil. When gypsum is transparent, like the sample shown here, it is called celestite.*

# Chapter 4

# Warm Shallow Seas —Where Rocks Were Built

During the Paleozoic Era, sea level around the planet rose several times. Seawater covered most continental crust, including Laurentia's. The level of the sea may have risen for several reasons. Perhaps there was a period during which more lava poured out of the seafloor-spreading zones than usual. Or perhaps continental crust sank a bit into the asthenosphere. This is the upper, more flexible part of the mantle. Or, perhaps the ice from an early ice age had melted.

Whatever happened, these rising sea waters were not sudden catastrophes. They probably rose slowly and moved inland at a rate of not more than a few inches each hundred years. But once in place, the water remained over the continental rock for much longer periods. When you read that a fossil animal developed in Laurentia's "warm shallow seas," these are the seas being talked about. They were warm at the time because Laurentia was lying across the equator.

The periods of shallow seas flooding the land played a major role in the development of Laurentia. First, they were the place where sediment settled after being eroded from the higher land. There were as yet no plants growing on the land. As a result, there was no protective cover that would prevent rocks from being eroded by wind and rain.

Second, warm shallow seas made excellent environments for growth. Plants and animals multiplied and developed quickly there. Sunlight easily penetrated such shallow seas. This allowed algae to grow. These plants provided food for animals. Many of the animals were shelled. Their shells added to the sediment. Sometimes entire shells were preserved as fossils. More often, the shells were broken into bits.

The first of the shallow Laurentian seas was called the Sauk Sea. This sea began to form even before the Cambrian Period. Life developed in this sea in great abundance. Even today, numerous marine fossils are found a long way inland in North America, far from today's oceans. There are no fossils of land-living life from the Cambrian Period, however. This indicates that living things had not yet made their way onto dry land.

*Sedimentary rock in Canyonlands National Park formed in a shallow sea and is now heavily eroded.*

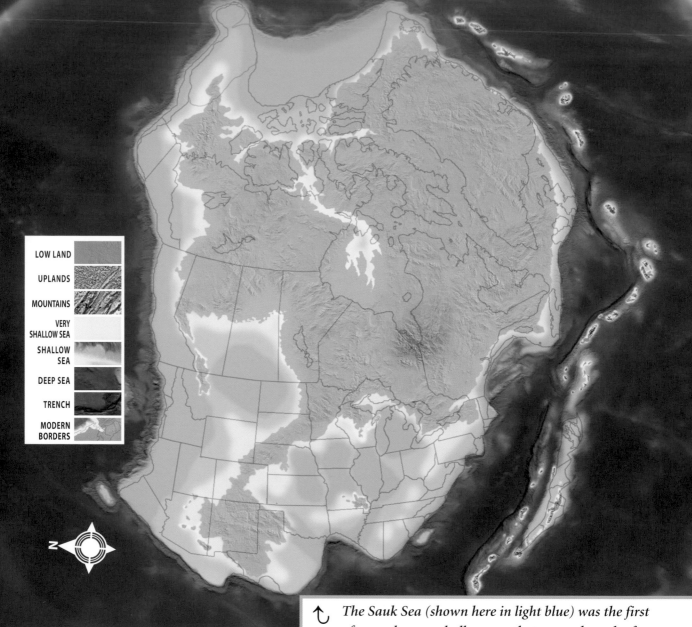

LOW LAND

UPLANDS

MOUNTAINS

VERY
SHALLOW SEA

SHALLOW
SEA

DEEP SEA

TRENCH

MODERN
BORDERS

*The Sauk Sea (shown here in light blue) was the first of several warm shallow seas that covered much of Laurentia. About 500 million years ago, it provided an environment in which marine life could develop*

The Sauk and later seas were probably not calm seas. Instead, they were often stirred by currents and waves caused by hurricane winds. The violent movement of the water eroded the softer rock underneath. The winds eroded rock on land. This eroded material—sediment—was churned around. It always settled in low spots. It built up both on the continent itself and on the continental shelf, the underwater part of the continent.

*This sandstone shows that the sediments forming it sometimes accumulated at angles to the regular rock beds.* ↱

## Sediments into Rocks

Sediment doesn't always settle smoothly. Geologists examine the way the layers of sedimentary rock formed. This helps them to analyze the ways that rivers flowed. Geologists can even determine what the weather was like over long periods of time.

The Sauk Sea covered almost the entire craton in what would become the United States. Only a few elevated areas were left exposed. These areas continued to erode and their sediments built up. Instead of sediment deriving only from rock, as we'll see in the next chapter, sediment also began to derive from living things.

The sediments that settle in water are gradually cemented together. This happens through the actions of various chemicals that enter water. Deep down, sheer pressure can cement them together. However the process happens, the result is rock. Rocks that form out of sediment tend to be of three different types: shales and mudstones, sandstones, and **limestones**. All might contain fossils.

*Shale is just hardened clay. As it hardened, it readily preserved fossilized traces of living things.* ↱

Shales are sedimentary rocks. They consist of layers of silt (very fine sand) mixed with mud. Shales easily separate into thin layers. If there is more mud than silt in the mix, the result is mudstone. Mudstone does not separate into layers. The Burgess Shale fossils formed in the sands of the Cambrian Period. They were protected from decay because mud quickly covered the soft animal bodies.

# Eroded by the Sauk Sea

In central Wisconsin, the Wisconsin River cuts through rock. This rock was formed in the Lower Paleozoic Era. The rock is mainly coarse sandstone with very few fossils. The sand cemented in the rock consists almost entirely of quartz sand grains. These were eroded from Precambrian rock by the currents within the shallow Sauk Sea. The sand settled, but the sediment did not form horizontal layers. Instead, currents in the water formed **cross-bedding**. A cross-bedded rock layer formed at a different angle from the regular horizontal layers of sediment. Cross-bedding indicates that the water carrying the sediment was flowing instead of still. The impression of these currents can still be seen in the rocks of today.

The area has become a center of tourism. People come to see the dramatic beauty of the rock formations along the river.

# Sandstone

Sandstone is a rock, but it is not necessarily solid. If you rub your hand across it, grains of sand separate. This fact means that sandstone is easily eroded. From the time it was formed, the Precambrian rock of the craton was exposed to erosion. Wind, rain, and running water all wore the rock away. The result was immense amounts of loose sand. Water and gravity carried the sand to lower and lower elevations until it could go no farther. It was deposited everywhere possible—along Laurentia's continental margins, in basins, and in riverbeds.

There are huge deposits of sandstone in the central western United States. The Native Americans who lived at Mesa Verde, Colorado, dug their homes and villages out of sandstone cliffs. Most of the magnificent red rock of the Southwest is red sandstone.

The sand of this period was primarily from the silica mineral called quartz. After the middle of the Paleozoic Era, sand became more varied. Different kinds of rocks contributed to it.

# Seas and Sands of the Grand Canyon

The Grand Canyon in northern Arizona features spectacular and deep walls of rock. The rock itself was formed during the Paleozoic Era. However, the canyon itself was not dug by the Colorado River until much later.

The rock at the bottom of the Grand Canyon is of Precambrian age. It was formed almost 1 billion years ago. The rock was uplifted and became the core of ancient mountains. The mountains were then worn down to a nearly flat surface. Younger sedimentary rock layers were deposited on the eroded surface. This created a break in the layers. Such a break is called an **unconformity**.

↵ The Great Unconformity

There are many unconformities in the Grand Canyon. One is so large that it is called the Great Unconformity. The rocks below the Great Unconformity are more than 1.5 billion years old, and they are tilted. Those above are almost a billion years younger. All of the rock lying between the Great Unconformity and the canyon's rim is seen in horizontal layers. The layers show that seas covered the area during the Paleozoic. Such sedimentary rocks as shales, limestones, and sandstones are of shallow marine or coastal origin.

The sea would retreat and then another would come in. Each time, the sediments deposited in the rock layers of the canyon were different.

The layers can be identified by color and content. For example, the 250-million-year-old Kaibab limestone contains many fossils. These include brachiopods and mollusks. The Coconino sandstone is 10 million years older. It is made of pure sand, with no fossils. The Supai Formation was formed about 285 million years ago and is different at each end. The eastern end of the formation was probably on land. It contains the fossils of land plants and animals. The western end was under the sea and contains marine fossils.

The overlying rock layers of the Grand Canyon are all of sedimentary origin. They do not record a continuous time of deposition, however. Layers from some time periods, such as the Ordovician Period, are missing. Perhaps there was nothing deposited during that time. Or perhaps whatever sediment was deposited eroded away before the next layer built up.

Permian

Pennsylvanian

Mississippian

Cambrian

Precambrian

## THE SCIENCE OF
## Limestone from the Ocean

Seawater contains **ions**. These are atoms or molecules that are missing an electron or have an extra electron. Ions have a positive or negative electrical charge. A complete atom is electrically neutral. It has no charge. Because of their charges, positive ions are drawn to negative ions. These then form electrically neutral atoms.

Among the ions in seawater are calcium ions and carbonate ions. Calcium ions are positive and carbonate ions are negative. When they join up, they form the mineral calcium carbonate, also called calcite. Chemically, this reaction is written:

$$Ca^{2+} + CO_3^{2-} \rightarrow CaCO_3$$

1 calcium ion + 1 carbonate ion makes 1 calcium carbonate (calcite) molecule

# Limestone

The rock called limestone is basically the chemical calcium carbonate mixed with sediments or mud. The calcium carbonate can come from two different sources. It can be derived from the ocean water itself. It can also come from living things that produce the chemical.

An important part of limestone derived from living things consists of reefs. These underwater rock structures were constructed long ago from the calcite shells of several kinds of animals. These animals included sponges, **bryozoans**, and corals. The shells were cemented together by a type of algae called **corraline**. Such algae produce calcium carbonate in their tissues.

During the Paleozoic, huge areas of reefs built up throughout the future Midwest of North America. Huge quantities of reef limestone are mined for building stone in Indiana, south of Chicago, Illinois.

# Silurian Limestone of Niagara Falls

The spectacular waterfall called Niagara Falls lies in both New York and Canada on the St. Lawrence River. Water from the Niagara River has been falling over the falls for more than 12,000 years. The rock of most falls would have worn away in that length of time. But the Niagara River flows over hard Silurian rock. This rock is too hard to easily erode.

The rushing water flows over a thick layer of Silurian limestone. The sandstone and shale under the limestone erode at a much faster rate. As the underlying rock erodes, blocks of limestone break off the ledge. These blocks drop to the base of the falls. The face of the falls remains nearly vertical, but it is now a few feet farther upstream. The falls' face has retreated this way regularly, gradually carving a spectacular gorge about 7 miles (11 km) long.

The same hard, raised Silurian limestone forms a long curving line across eastern North America. It curves from New York, below Lake Ontario, over northern Michigan, and down into Wisconsin along Lake Michigan. Along most of its length, the Silurian rock is not exposed, as it is at Niagara Falls.

The Silurian limestone contains many fossils of **invertebrates**, or animals without backbones. New York State even has an official state fossil, the eurypterid. This is a type of Silurian arthropod called a sea scorpion.

# Turning Off the Falls

The American side of Niagara Falls was actually "turned off" for several months in 1969. Much of the American side of the falls had fallen away as the limestone broke. It was lying in heaps at the bottom of the falls. The United States was in danger of losing this famed site. The U.S. Army Corps of Engineers stopped the flow of the falls. They redirected the Niagara River over to the Canadian side of the falls. Meanwhile, Corps engineers studied the problem. They finally decided that they would let nature take its own course. Niagara Falls was "turned" back on.

Some of the earliest plants contain skeletonlike structures made of calcium carbonate. This is perhaps because of the amount of calcium carbonate in the ocean. The bodies of many early marine animals also evolved to construct shells out of the mineral. The remains of these plants and animal shells formed the bulk of the sediment making up limestone.

Many calcite shells made by marine animals are pretty and interesting, especially to shell collectors. One of the most unusual calcite formations is the pearl. A pearl begins as an irritation within an oyster's shell. When a grain of sand gets under its shell, the oyster may gradually wall off the irritation. It does this by secreting calcite from carbonate and calcium ions. It builds a beautiful wall around the grain of sand or other irritant.

*The outer shell, the sparkly lining, called mother-of-pearl, and the pearl itself are all made of alcite, which the oyster secretes.* ↻

# Bending and Breaking Rock Layers

Sedimentary layers of rock may not always remain the same. Pressure on Earth's crust can be exerted from hundreds of miles away. This pressure can slowly force distant layers of rock to bend or fracture. These events are called **deformations**. Bending can create rock structures called **folds**. These form as arched patterns in the rock layers. Folding on a gigantic scale can create mountains.

*This fold in layers of sedimentary rock was exposed when a road was cut through the rock.*

*This fault, or break, happened when the pressure on the sedimentary layers was too great for the rock to just fold.*

Faults are fractures, or breaks, in the layers. They occur when the continuing pressure becomes too great. The layers of rock then break, instead of just bending. The rock on each side of a fault can be moved, or displaced, in different directions. This faulting causes earthquakes. Earthquakes may move the rock on either side great distances. Faulting that moves rock upward is a main cause of mountain building.

## Deformations in Sedimentary Rock in Utah

Central Utah has thin soil and little vegetation. Rock layers therefore can easily be seen in this part of the state.

Sedimentary rock layers normally appear as one horizontal layer deposited on top of others. The rock layers would then read upward—like pages in a book describing a history of Earth.

The sedimentary rock layers in central Utah were deposited over vast expanses of land. The layers show evidence of disturbance. A disturbance can break, or fracture, the rock. If the rock on each side of a fracture moves, the disturbance is a fault. A large fault line can be seen in the photo below. Note how far apart the two sections of the dark line are.

Displacement or movement of the rock layers also is evident. The rock to the left of the fault line moved upward and to the right. This can be seen especially when compared to the other side. The horizontal expanse of the rock has decreased. This indicates that the rock has also been compressed.

Rock layers at the bottom of this canyon in central Utah have been tilted almost vertically. More horizontal layers lie on top. This unconformity was created after the rock was tilted. Erosion formed a nearly horizontal surface along the tilted layers. Horizontal rock layers were then deposited on top of the eroded surface. The upper layers do not match, or conform to, the lower layers. Pages in that part of Earth history are missing in the rock.

# Warm Shallow Seas —Where Life Evolved

During the Precambrian Period of Earth's geological history, continents formed and reformed. The ancient supercontinent called Rodinia broke into two main parts, Pannotia and Siberia. Then Pannotia split into three more continents. These continents then drifted apart.

Gondwana was by far the biggest of the three continents. It remained a supercontinent until 130 million years ago. This supercontinent included Australia, India, South America, Africa, and Antarctica. Pannotia's two other continents were the smaller lands called Baltica and Laurentia, or North America.

Around each of the newly separated continents was a continental shelf. This underwater crust gradually slopes downward to meet the oceanic crust. Marine life developed on the continental shelves.

The Sauk Sea helped create the Cambrian explosion of life. This sea was only the first of several great shallow seas that covered much of the continents. These seas flowed in and out over Laurentia during the Paleozoic Era as a result of changes in sea level.

These major changes in sea level brought about major changes in marine life. Most of the important classes of marine invertebrates developed during the early Paleozoic Era. But something equally important happened as a result of the changes. These sea-level changes killed off, or made extinct, many existing species of living things.

There were three **mass extinctions** of living things during the Paleozoic. These occurred at the end of the Ordovician, during the late Devonian, and at the end of the Permian. Paleontologists estimate that 27 percent of the families of living things and 57 percent of **genera** became extinct at the end of the Ordovician. Almost that many were extinguished during the late Devonian when the shallow seas pulled back into the ocean.

*A museum exhibit shows what life was probably like in a shallow Ordovician sea.*

# Early Paleozoic Communities

Not many different species made up the communities of living things in the sea during the Cambrian, or even throughout the entire Paleozoic. The extraordinary variety of life that we know today did not develop until during the Mesozoic Era.

As holds true today, life depended on plants that could produce their own food. The process plants use to produce their own food is called **photosynthesis**. The primary early plants were algae. These are mostly single-celled simple plants. Some algae may be long, thin, ribbonlike plants. They stretch from the seafloor to near the surface of the sea. Others may be microscopic in size. Microscopic algae make up a large part of the **plankton** that supports other marine life. *Plankton* is the name given to the living things that freely float with ocean currents. Marine life feed on these plants and animals.

Plankton is made up in part of a large group of single-celled animals called **foraminiferans**, or forams. These **protozoans** began appearing during the Cambrian. They evolved into many different forms by the Devonian. Most early animals had shells on the outside of their soft bodies. But some forams had a shell, called a test, inside the body. Even today, foram tests make up a large part of the ooze on the bottom of the sea.

↰ *Plankton* (top) *and foraminiferans* (bottom) *are single-celled organisms that served as important foods for other marine animals during the Paleozoic, as they still do today.*

52

# The Important Algae

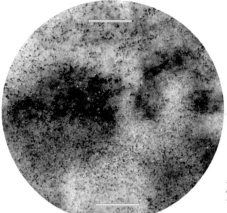

↥ Red algae in snow

Algae are simple plants. They are capable of photosynthesis. This means they produce their own food. Algae live in a wide variety of environments. They are found in the cold of ice and snow, the temperate waters of lakes and seas, and even in the boiling water of hot springs. Many different animals feed upon algae.

The first algae were single-celled plants. Such plants began to carry on photosynthesis during the Precambrian. Algae combine carbon dioxide and water to produce food. A waste product of the process is oxygen. The process of photosynthesis thus resulted in oxygen being added to Earth's atmosphere. Marine animal life developed during the Cambrian. This marine life was dependent on the algae in plankton for food.

Green algae are often seen as fine strands of plant life. These strands form the floating scum on ponds. Red algae are usually marine. They produce calcium carbonate, which makes them an important part of reef building. The algae often called seaweeds are usually brown algae, such as kelp. These can form large "forests" of algae in shallow seas. No matter what their color, all algae are really green plants that carry on photosynthesis. The green color is masked by other colors.

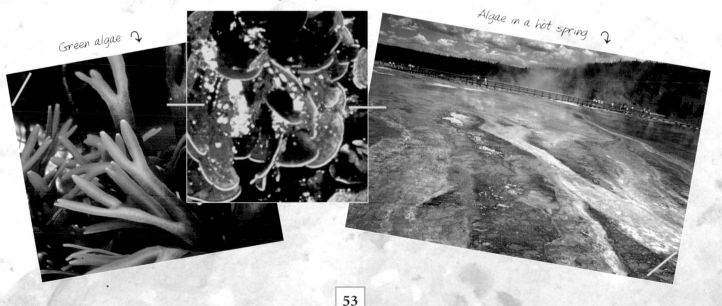

Green algae ↘    Brown algae ↘    Algae in a hot spring ↘

↻ *Sponges come in many shapes, sizes, and colors. Their shape is formed by silica.*

The primary animal forms larger than protozoans during the Cambrian were trilobites and sponges. Perhaps half of all animals at that time were trilobites. That does not mean that there were not animals from many other groups, or phyla. Most phyla that are known today got their start during this period. Their members were not the only ones that laid down fossils, however. Other vast quantities of fossils were laid down. These would also make up much of North American rock some day.

Sponges are readily found in Cambrian rock. They may have existed before then, however. Fossilized spikes of the mineral silica identify these simple animals. This mineral gave form to their soft, porous bodies. One group of sponges that is extinct today combined with algae to build reefs.

## The Main Inhabitants of Paleozoic Seas

During the first part of the Paleozoic, new groups of shelled invertebrate animals developed. Shells provided support for the animals' soft bodies. These soft bodies had no skeletons. With the external support of shells, these animals could evolve to grow larger. Shells also prevented the animals' soft bodies from drying out. In addition, shells protected the animals from predators that were also evolving. Predators stalking the sea at the time included cephalopods such as squids and large trilobites.

Unlike trilobites, most new animals were unable to move around. They occupied permanent positions with a body part attached to a rock. They ate whatever plankton happened to come their way.

The animals called brachiopods had larvae, which were shell-less young forms, that could swim freely. As they grew, though, they developed shells that became attached to rocks on the seafloor. Brachiopods look somewhat like clams. Clams and brachiopods are not related, however. Their internal structures are quite different. Brachiopods have feathery tentacles that send food to the mouth. Clams have siphons, which are organs shaped like tubes that suck in food.

Numerous species of brachiopods occupied many different kinds of environments. These animals still exist, mainly in cold water.

↳ *Cambrian brachiopod fossils*

## Ordovician Life

The beginning of the Cambrian saw the development of many new types of animals. The same is true of the beginning of the next period, the Ordovician. This sudden appearance of new types of animals is sometimes called the Ordovician radiation. No one knows for sure why this rapid expansion of animal life took place. When scientists talk about "Paleozoic fauna," they are usually referring to animals that developed as part of the Ordovian radiation. A museum exhibit of Ordovician life is shown on pages 50 and 51.

**Bryozoans** are sometimes called moss animals. This is because they form mosslike crusts on rocks and ship bottoms. In fact, for many centuries they were thought to be plants. They are actually animals, however. Bryozoans are tiny. They are not much more than a millimeter in size. The colonies, or reefs, they formed may cover vast areas, however. This animal phylum is unusual because it does not appear in the fossil record until the Ordovician.

↳ *Bryozoans, or moss animals, did not appear until the Ordovician.*

Thousands of species of bryozoans colonized the seafloors of the Paleozoic. This stationary animal somewhat resembles coral. It has a more complex body structure, however. Like coral, bryozoans form colonies. They may even build reefs. The soft-bodied bryozoan secretes an exoskeleton that takes the shape of a tube or box. These exoskeletons become attached to each other and may take on a variety of different forms. Thus bryozoan colonies may be described by such terms as branching, encrusting, lacy, and netlike.

**Echinoderms** also developed during the Cambrian. They did not become prominent until the Ordovician, however. Today, these animals are represented by starfish and sea urchins. The name *echinoderm* means "spiny skin." These animals had spines projecting through the exoskeleton. These spines made them look almost like flowers.

The most prominent echinoderms to form fossils were crinoids. Today, they are known as sea lilies. Their stems made them look like plants. The stems consisted of plates of calcite.

↳ *A fossilized branching colony of bryozoans*

↳ *Living starfish in a tide pool are little different from the echinoderms that became common during the Ordovician.*

# Flowers on the Seafloor

Although crinoids are not plants, they are often called sea lilies. Crinoids are marine animals that were abundant in the Paleozoic. They are closely related to sea stars. Crinoids resemble sea stars attached to the seafloor by long stems.

The body of a crinoid contains the animal's vital organs. Its arms appear in multiples of five, as they do in all echinoderms. The arms are attached to the body. They direct food particles toward the mouth. The mouth opens upward from the central body. A stem anchors the crinoid to the seafloor for its entire adult life.

Complete crinoid fossils are somewhat rare. They are normally found as broken parts making up large masses of limestone. This is a fossilized crinoid body (left) and a section of broken stem (right).

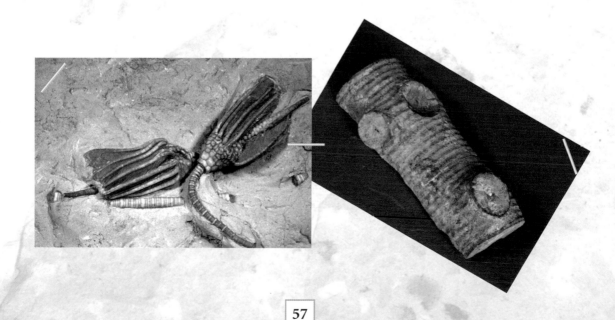

> *Today's nautilus (right) is a descendant of the much larger predatory **nautiloids** (above), which began prowling the seas during the Ordovician.*

# Moving off the Bottom of the Sea

The evolution of living things allowed new species to take advantage of more habitats. The first marine animals, for example, lived only on the seafloor or burrowed into it. During the Ordovician Period, the long-stemmed crinoids reached up into a higher level. They reached perhaps several feet off the seafloor. At that level they could take advantage of any plankton that flowed past.

Free-swimming animals developed, too. Mollusks (shellfish) vary from snails to clams to oysters to squid. Thousands of new species of mollusk developed during the Ordovician. Most prominent were the group called cephalopods. This name literally means "head foot."

Cephalopods called nautiloids resembled today's nautilus. They were not coiled, however. They were predators that looked like squids in long, cone-shaped shells.

The soft body of the nautiloid occupied only one section at the end of the shell. The remainder was divided into chambers. These chambers could be emptied or filled with air. This change would make the animal sink or rise in the water.

Cephalopods would not reach the peak of their development until the Devonian Period. At that time, the newer ammonites developed. They might be 6 feet (1.8 m) long. These ammonites remained vicious marine predators until the end of the Mesozoic Era. At that time, they died out with the dinosaurs. Ammonites can be useful as index fossils. This is because many of the species existed for a specific, known time period.

*Colonies of tiny graptolites are known primarily from their carbonized fossils. This graptolite fossil is from the Silurian Period.*

# New Animals with Backbones

Graptolites are animals that represent a stage between invertebrates and **vertebrates**. Invertebrates are animals without backbones. Vertebrates are animals with backbones. Graptolites are often found as fossils. These look like narrow tubes with tiny, toothed structures projecting out from the full length of the tube. They probably floated with the currents in the Ordovician and Silurian seas. Graptolites formed useful index fossils.

For many years, paleontologists found groups of microscopic teeth in Ordovician rock. These were assumed to be the teeth of some vertebrate. Then, in 1995, a complete fossil of a minnow-shaped eely animal was found. This fossil was called a conodont. It had no backbone, but it did have the beginnings of a cord of nerves in its back. This cord was the ancestor of a spinal cord and backbone.

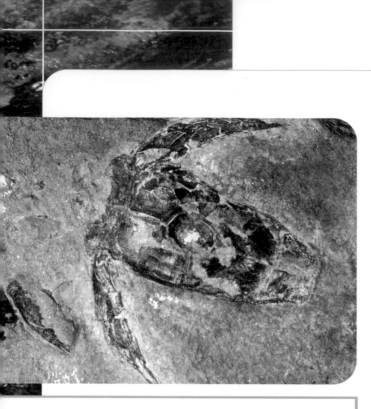

The earliest vertebrates are visible in Cambrian rocks. Their fossils are scattered and fragmentary, however. Complete fossilized animals with backbones don't appear until the Ordovician Period. These were jawless fishes. They are usually described as "armored." This is because they had hard shields covering their heads. These first vertebrates grazed on algae.

The jawless fishes had skeletons made of **cartilage** instead of bone. Cartilage is the hard but flexible material in your nose and ears. Today's jawless fishes include only the lamprey and hagfish.

The development of vertebrates was an amazing process. Also amazing is the fact that these jawless fishes could survive in freshwater instead of salty seawater. This development was possible when numerous habitats became available. Fishes began to develop rapidly, especially during the Silurian Period.

↺ *The jawless fishes (above) were the first true vertebrates, animals with backbones. One of the few jawless fishes remaining today is the lamprey . Its sucking "mouth" is shown here (below).*

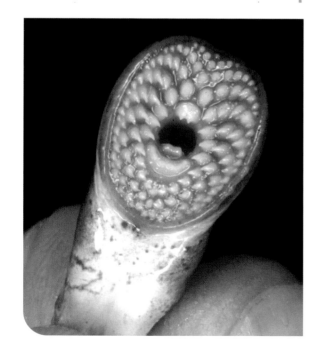

## The Move from Water to Land

Some individual marine animals may have moved onto the land for short periods of time. This includes mollusks and arthropods—especially millipede-like animals. Perhaps they were searching for food. However, it wasn't until the late Ordovician Period, maybe 450 million years ago, that some primitive animals stayed on the land. They began to develop into animals that were able to live their entire lives on land.

## HOW DO THEY KNOW
### All Vertebrates Are Related?

The same amount of salt (sodium chloride) is found in the blood of all vertebrates. This includes birds, amphibians, reptiles, fish, and mammals. The salt content is the same as seawater that has been diluted to one-fourth of its natural saltiness. This fact makes biologists believe that vertebrates developed when the sea was one-fourth as saline, or salty, as it is now. This would have been the case during the Paleozoic Era. It is this salt in the blood that also allowed animals to move to freshwater from saltwater. They carried the salt their bodies needed with them.

Movement onto land was one of the biggest changes that living things made during the early Paleozoic Era. It wasn't easy for water-living creatures (both plant and animal) to make this move. They had to give up the advantages that water gave them. Water helped them fight gravity, maintain body shape, find food, and reproduce.

Moving onto land resulted in changes in plants. They acquired leaves, which provided a large surface for sun to strike, increasing photosynthesis. With increased food making by photosynthesis, plants grew faster.

The movement of plants onto land also resulted in changes in the land itself. An important change was that when crustal rock was covered by plants, it could no longer be eroded so easily. The erosion of sediment slowed down.

*Plants acquired large leaves for life on land.*

When a huge ice cap forms, such as on Antarctica, the water to build the ice comes from the ocean. The buildup of such ice on Gondwana probably contributed to the Ordovician extinction.

The Ordovician extinction was probably caused by the location of Gondwana. This massive supercontinent was near the South Pole. When the temperature of Earth dropped, huge glaciers formed over the land. The water needed to form this huge ice cap came from the ocean. So sea levels dropped, and the shallow seas that had covered Laurentia receded. Many animals could not survive this change in both temperature and sea level. Their species became extinct, or their numbers shrank so much that they are not often found as fossils.

*This fossil-bearing limestone was formed during the Ordovician Period. At the end of that period, the number of animals that might have made fossils dropped greatly.*

# Silurian Life

In general, those animal species that survived the Ordovician extinction lived in the colder seas at high latitudes. New species arose and quickly became dominant, however. The seas rose again as the glaciers of Gondwana melted. Major reefs developed again. This time, however, they were built by coral animals.

*A museum display of a Silurian coral reef shows that many different marine animals took advantage of the food supplies on the reef.*

# A Modern Coral Reef

The coral is a soft-bodied marine animal called a **polyp** and the hard enclosing tube of calcite that it secretes around itself. When corals live in a colony, an underwater reef of limestone may be formed when their calcite shells, or corallites, become cemented together.

Coral reefs were huge during the middle of the Paleozoic Era. Much of the Midwest of the United States and Canada is made of limestone formed by corals at that time.

Coral reefs are still found in warm shallow seas. The reefs form the basis for large communities of life. These communities include algae, a great number of invertebrates, and fishes. In North America, coral reefs are found off the southern coast of Florida. The reefs extend southward into the Caribbean Sea.

↖ Coral polyps have tentacles surrounding the mouth.

↖ A coral reef supports a wide variety of life.

True corals appeared during the Ordovician Period. They survived to become very important during the Silurian Period. Corals belong to the same phylum as jellyfish and sea anemones. The actual coral animal, called a polyp, secretes a hard calcite shell. The shell, called a corallite, is usually tube-shaped. The corallites are cemented together by calcium carbonate secreted by the algae known as corallines.

Coral reefs formed in the shallow seas. Here they often became barriers around quiet lagoons that protected the land

*Fringing reefs form near islands in shallow tropical waters. They protect the land from wave action.*

from the ocean waves. In such places, living things could develop in relative safety. The reefs of the Silurian and Devonian were very like today's reefs.

The first plant to move into freshwater from saltwater was probably a type of green algae. After these plants made that transition, they moved onto land. The first land plants seem to have appeared during the Silurian Period, though they may have appeared earlier.

These first land plants were very simple. They reproduced by spores, which are much like pollen. Unlike pollen, they have tough walls that withstand being in the air. Spores need water to keep from drying out. As a result, these plants tended to live near swamps. Plants with protective seed coverings developed later.

Plants could not live on land until they developed veins. The veins move water throughout the plant. The stem of a plant with these veins can stand erect on land. This is because it has water in its tissues. These plants are called **vascular** plants. The first ones have been found in Silurian rocks. These plants were very small and had no leaves or real roots.

# The 400 Million-Year-Old Legged Fish

Certain Silurian fishes eventually became land vertebrates. Among these were a group called **crossopterygians**. Their fins had bones in them. These bones supported them when they moved onto land. These strange fishes were probably the ancestors of amphibians.

The ancient crossopterygians were all assumed to be extinct. Then, in 1938, a fisherman from South Africa pulled up a fish he didn't recognize. A local museum thought the fish was very strange. It set about having it identified. After more than a year, the fish was recognized as being "the most important zoological find of the century." Fourteen more years passed before an additional specimen was found. This discovery was an ancient crossopterygian called a coelacanth (SEE-luh-canth). Since then, more "living fossils" have been caught in African waters.

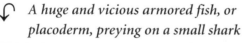

*A huge and vicious armored fish, or placoderm, preying on a small shark*

Fishes also continued to change during the Silurian Period. The first fishes with jaws developed about 410 million years ago. This particular type of fish, called a spiny shark, was extinct by the end of the Paleozoic.

The first fishes with skeletons made of bone instead of cartilage appeared soon after the jawed fishes. This probably occurred during the Silurian Period. No fossils of bony fishes from that time have been found in marine sediments, however. Perhaps they developed in freshwater, in the mouths of rivers.

*Marine life was greatly diversified during the Devonian, as shown by this museum display.*

# Devonian Life

The Devonian Period has been called the Age of Fishes. There had been jawless fishes around since the Cambrian Period. During the Devonian, however, many new advanced types of fishes appeared. These fishes brought great diversity to the vertebrates.

An early type of jawed fish was called a placoderm. It was a vicious predator of the sea. This placoderm reached 30 feet (9 m) in length. It had heavy armor covering its head and body. There were perhaps 200 species of placoderm. Most became extinct at the end of the Devonian. Placoderm descendants, however, led to today's modern fishes.

*Large predators and many other kinds of fishes developed during the Devonian, called the Age of Fishes.*

## Reefs and Oil

A mile beneath the ground in Western Canada are the remains of vast coral reefs. These were built during the Devonian Period. For millions of years, the remains of the living things in the reef fell into the reef basin and accumulated. Fine-grained sediments also settled in the basin. Together, the grains and the once-living material formed shale. Pressure from above forced the shale into holes in the reef. Over many millions of years, the reefs were fossilized. The once-living remains changed into petroleum and natural gas. This is why petroleum and natural gas are called fossil fuels. The oil in Western Canada was found in 1947. The discovery of oil turned Alberta, Canada, into one of the major oil-producing areas of North America.

↰ *Trilobites and nautiloids were very different from each other.*

Arthropods such as trilobites developed, as we have seen, early in the Cambrian Period. Other arthropods, insects, also developed. Insects do not make very good fossils. Therefore, their early evolution is uncertain. The first certain fossils of insects were found in Devonian rock. They were tiny and wingless. They developed wings and spread in great numbers later in the Paleozoic Era. Insects developed into the most successful phylum of all animals.

Toward the end of the Devonian Period, some vertebrates moved to land. Their bodies had to develop different ways of dealing with their new environment.

# The Devonian at the Falls of the Ohio

One of the best fossil beds in the world is found along the Falls of the Ohio River in extreme southern Indiana. The fossils here are those of life that existed in the coral reef communities of Devonian time. The fossils are found in limestone that includes the tangled remains of corals, sponges, brachiopods, mollusks, crinoids, and other marine life.

  Although the Falls of the Ohio River is far from any present-day sea and its climate is not tropical today, the fossil beds indicate that tropical seas must have covered this area during the Devonian Period.

↵ Limestone from the Falls of the Ohio River reveals many holes in which tiny animals once lived.

An unusual sphere of ↷ fossilized chain coral

69

*The lobe-finned crossopterygian fish had muscled fins that let them walk on land. They also had lungs as well as gills, which let them breathe out of water. They developed into amphibians.*

The crossopterygians developed legs and specialized gills. These gills could use oxygen from the atmosphere instead of from water. These animals became a new type of vertebrate, amphibians. Like the frogs, toads, and salamanders of today, they were still tied to water. This is because they had to lay their eggs in water. Some of the earliest amphibians were as much as 6 feet (2 m) long.

After vascular plants developed during the Silurian Period, they grew rapidly. They had tubes to transport water up the stem. This allowed plants to produce wood. Vascular plants went from small bog plants to forests of giant trees. This happened in less than 50 million years, within the Devonian Period.

## The Oldest Fossil Trees

The world's oldest fossil forest has been found in New York's Catskill Mountains. Called the Gilboa Forest, it was discovered in 1869 after a flash flood washed away the overlying sediment that had covered the fossil forest. The forest consists of the stumps of trees that grew during the Devonian Period. Such trees are the ancestors of today's evergreens. They grew in mud by the edge of a sea. The mud turned to shale. The stumps visible today are actually casts of the original trees, which have long since rotted away.

About 90 million years had passed since the beginning of the Paleozoic Era. The small continents of Laurentia and Baltica collided. They formed a larger continent often called Laurussia. An amazing number and range of living things developed during those 90 million years.

A large number of the species that had appeared were about to disappear. This is because the end of the Devonian brought another mass extinction. Global cooling was probably the cause. It affected the life in the warm shallow seas that had once again spread across much of the continental surface.

The destruction was mainly suffered by the huge reef communities and other marine life. It did not affect the growing diversity of land plants. These plants would play an important role in the second half of the Paleozoic Era.

*At the end of the Devonian Period, plants had taken over the land. Large marine animals were beginning to join them.*

# GEOLOGIC TIME SCALE

| Time Period | Tectonic Events | Biological Events |
|---|---|---|
| **Hadean Eon** *4.5–3.96 billion years ago* Named for Hades, or Hell | No Earth rocks from this time found | None |
| **Archean Eon** *3.96–2.5 billion years ago* Name means "Ancient" | Oldest known rocks First permanent crust First stable continents | Seawater formed First bacteria Atmosphere formed |
| **Proterozoic Eon** *2.5 billion–543 million* | North American craton formed First iron–bearing sediments First large glaciation Formation and breakup of Rodinia supercontinent Gondwana, southern supercontinent, formed | Free oxygen in atmosphere First nucleated cells, allowing sexual reproduction First multicellular animals First animals with exoskeletons First fungi |

PHANEROZOIC TIME • 543 million years ago to present

PALEOZOIC ERA • 543 to 248 million years ago

| Time Period | Tectonic Events | Biological Events |
|---|---|---|
| **Cambrian Period** *543–248 million years ago* Named for old name of Wales | Laurentia separated from Siberia | Cambrian Explosion: Major diversification of marine invertebrates |
| **Ordovician Period** *490–443 million years ago* Named for a Celtic tribe in Wales | First Iapetus Ocean Taconic orogeny in northeastern Laurentia | First true vertebrates: jawless fish First land plants Mass extinction |
| **Silurian Period** *443–417 million years ago* Named for a Celtic tribe in Wales | Caledonian orogeny Shallow seas on Laurentia | First vascular plants First insects First jawed fish |
| **Devonian Period** *417–354 million years ago* Named for Devon, England | Major reef building | First forests First seed–baring plants First four–footed animals First amphibians |
| CARBONIFEROUS PERIOD 354 to 290 million years ago · **Mississippian Epoch** *354–323 million years ago* Named for Mississippi River Valley | Antler orogeny | Ferns abundant First land vertebrates |
| **Pennsylvanian Epoch** *323–290 million years ago* Named for coal formations in Pennsylvania | Appalachian orogeny began Antler orogeny | Ferns abundant Major coal–forming forests First reptiles |
| **Permian** *290–248 million years ago* Named for Russian province of Perm | Pangea formed | First warm–blooded reptiles Greatest mass extinction |

| | Time Period | Tectonic Events | Biological Events |
|---|---|---|---|
| **MESOZOIC ERA** *248 to 65 million years ago* | **Triassic Period** *248–206 million years ago* Named for three layers in certain European rocks | Pangea completed Major part of Pangea was arid | First flying vertebrates First dinosaurs First mammals Cephalopods abundant |
| | **Jurassic Period** *206–144 million hears ago* Named for the Jura Mountains | Atlantic began to open Pangea separated into Gondwana and Laurasia | First birds Cycads abundant |
| | **Cretaceous Period** *144–65 million years ago* Named after Latin word for "chalk" | Major volcanism Sevier orogeny Laurentia separated from Eurasia Sierra Nevada batholith | First flowering plants First social insects Mass extinction of dinosaurs |

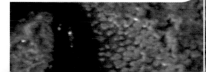

| | | Time Period | Tectonic Events | Biological Events |
|---|---|---|---|---|
| **PHANEROZOIC TIME • 543 million years ago to present** — **CENOZOIC ERA • 65 million years ago to present** | **TERTIARY PERIOD • 65 to 1.8 million years ago** | **Paleocene Epoch** *65 to 54.8 million years ago* | Laramide orogeny Western Laurentia uplifted | Mammals and birds diversified First horse ancestors |
| | | **Eocene Epoch** *54.8 to 33.7 million years ago* | Rockies uplifted Global cooling began | First mammals (whales) in sea First primates First cats and dogs |
| | | **Oligocene Epoch** *33.7 to 23.8 million years ago* | North Atlantic opened Ice cap formed in Anatarctica | First apes Grasslands widespread |
| | | **Miocene Epoch** *23.8 to 5.3 million years ago* | Columbia flood basalts | First human ancestors First mastodons |
| | | **Pliocene Epoch** *5.3 to 1.8 million years ago* | Northern Hemisphere glaciation began Cascade Volcanoes | Large mammals abundant |
| | **QUATERNARY PERIOD** *1.8 million to today* | **Pleistocene Epoch** *1.8 million years ago to today* | Great glaciation of Northern Hemisphere | First modern humans Extinction of large mammals Humans entered North America |
| | | **Holocene** *10,000 years ago to today* | Rifting continued in East Africa Human–caused global warming | Human-caused extinctions |

# GLOSSARY

**absolute time** dating of rocks and geologic events according to age in years. This is in contrast to relative time, which considers only the order of events.

**accretion** the addition of terrane to a larger tectonic plate; typically occurs by subduction.

**algae** (singular is **alga**) simple water-living plants, such as seaweed or pond scum, with natural green color often hidden by brown or red tint. Algae lack true roots, stems, or leaves.

**amber** hard yellow, red, or brown fossil resin of coniferous, or cone-bearing, trees. Ancient organisms were trapped in this resin and were preserved whole.

**ammonite** animal with a flat, coiled, chambered shell. This cephalopod mollusk dates from the Devonian to the Cretaceous. Some had long tentacles or arms.

**arthropod** animal with a jointed body and limbs and a segmented exoskeleton, including spiders and insects

**asthenosphere** the part of Earth's mantle that lies beneath the lithosphere. This zone of soft, easily changed, or deformed, rock is believed to be less rigid, hotter, and more fluid than rock above or below.

**bacteria** (singular is **bacterium**) tiny, one-celled organisms that can be seen only with a microscope

**basin** a low area, or depression, in the earth's surface where sediment collects.

**brachiopod** a shelled, clamlike marine animal without a backbone but with tentacles

**bryozoan** a freshwater or marine colonial animal. Also called moss animals, bryozoans form branching, encrusting, or jellylike masses that resemble moss. They live in colonies, or groups of their own kind. The adults anchor themselves to one location and make up reefs.

**calcite** mineral made of calcium carbonate ($CaCO_3$), which is the principal component of limestone and chalk. Many seashells are made of calcite.

**Canadian Shield** the largest area of exposed Precambrian rock on Earth. This ancient rock of the North American craton covers more than 1.8 million square miles (4.8 million sq km) from the Great Lakes to the Canadian Arctic to Greenland.

**carbonate** in minerals, a compound that contains the carbonate ion ($CO_3$). A carbonate rock is made primarily of carbonate minerals, such as limestone.

**cartilage** a stiff but flexible tissue that makes up the skeletons of some fishes

**cephalopod** a mollusk with tentacles attached to the head. Cephalopods include the squid, octopus, and nautilus. The name means "head foot."

**coralline** red algae that produces calcium carbonate in its tissues; the cement that holds reefs together

**core** the interior part of Earth beginning at about 1,800 miles (2,900 km) below Earth's surface. Composed mostly of iron and nickel, it is divided into two parts: the outer core, which is mostly liquid, and the inner core, which is solid.

**craton** the usually stable, unmovable mass of rock in Earth's crust that forms the central mass of a continent

**crinoid** an echinoderm that has a cup-shaped body with branched, radiating arms. Crinoids were common on the sea floor during the Paleozoic Era. Today they include sea lilies and feather stars.

**cross-bedding** rocks found at angles that differ from the regular angle, or bedding. Cross-bedding forms in moving water or on sand dunes.

**crossopterygian** mostly extinct lobe-finned fish that possessed lungs. They are the ancestors of amphibians and other land vertebrates.

**crust** the outermost, rocky layer of Earth. This low-density layer is about 22 miles (35 km) thick under continents and 6 mi (10 km) thick under oceans.

**deformation** the changes in shape, dimension, or volume of rocks that result from folding, faulting, and other processes

**echinoderm** any marine, invertebrate animal that has a five-part, radially symmetrical body. Echinoderms today include starfishes, sea urchins, sea cucumbers, and sea lilies.

**era** a division of geologic time next smaller than the eon and larger than a period. For example, the Paleozoic Era is in the Phanerozoic Eon and includes the Ordovician Period.

**evaporite** the mineral that remains after mineral-laden water has evaporated. Evaporites include rock salt (halite) and gypsum.

**evolution** the theory that all existing living things are related and that they developed from earlier forms of the organisms

**exoskeleton** outer skeleton. Shellfish, such as crabs and lobsters, and other arthropods have exoskeletons.

**exotic terrane** a piece of lithosphere caught between two plates as they crash together. See **terrane**.

**extinct** no longer in existence

**fault** a fracture in rock along which each side moves relative to the other. Sudden movements on fault lines are felt as earthquakes.

**fjord** a narrow passageway from the sea between cliffs or tall hills, often reaching deeply inland; generally caused by glaciers eroding the land

**fold** a noticeable curve in the layer of sedimentary or metamorphic rock. Large-scale folding of rock can create mountains.

**foraminiferans** marine protozoans with calcite shell. Also known as forams, they are are found in limestone and in the ooze on the ocean floor.

**fossil** evidence or trace of animal or plant life of a past geological age. These usually mineralized remains have been preserved in rocks of the earth's crust. Traces include bones and footprints of extinct land animals, such as dinosaurs.

**gastropod** type of mollusk with a coiled shell and a distinct head with eyes. Present-day gastropods are snails, slugs, and limpets. These move by means of a wide, muscular foot.

**genus** (plural is **genera**) a major subdivision in a biological family or subfamily in the classification of organisms. Genera usually are made up of more than one species.

**geologic time scale** the sequence of units of Earth time, in chronological order according to eras, periods, and epochs; see pages 72 and 73

**glacier** a mass of very dense ice on land that moves slowly, by coming down from high mountains or spreading out across land from a central point of accumulation

**Gondwana** supercontinent in the Southern Hemisphere that lasted more than half a billion years. Mostly a separate landmass, it was part of the bigger supercontinent Pangea until the end of the Paleozoic. It contained present-day South America, Africa, southern Europe, the peninsula of India, Australia, and Antarctica.

**granite** coarse-grained igneous rock composed primarily of sodium and potassium feldspar, but also rich in quartz

**gypsum** a soft mineral, hydrous calcium sulfate, which sometimes forms soft beds. Gypsum was one of the first minerals to form from evaporating water.

**halite** soft, grayish mineral, sodium chloride (NaCl), which is common table salt. Also known as rock salt, it is an evaporite that forms from evaporating water.

**igneous rock** rock formed directly from magma that has cooled and solidified. *Igneous* means "fiery."

**index fossil** any animal or plant fossil that is representative of a certain time period. Index fossils are well defined, easily identifiable, and plentiful. They are spread widely throughout an area during a relatively short range of time.

**invertebrate** an animal without a backbone or spinal column; not a vertebrate

**ion** an atom that is missing an electron, or has an extra electron. This electrically charged atom has a negative or a positive charge.

**island arc** a curved or arc-shaped chain of volcanic islands lying near a continent, formed as a result of subduction, such as the Aleutian Islands in Alaska

**Laurentia** a large continent formed during the Paleozoic Era from which the modern continent of North America developed. It was composed mostly of North America and Greenland, parts of northwestern Scotland and Scandinavia.

**lava** fluid molten rock, or magma, that emerges from a volcano or volcanic vent to the earth's surface. When cooled and solidified, it forms an igneous rock.

**limestone** a type of sedimentary rock, made up of more than 50% of calcium carbonate ($CaCO_3$), primarily as the mineral calcite, which may be mixed with sediments or mud

**lithosphere** the hard outer layer of Earth containing the outer part of Earth's mantle and its crust. It consists of tectonic plates that float on the asthenosphere.

**magma** molten rock that exists beneath the earth's crust. When this molten rock flows to the surface, it is called lava.

**mantle** the thick part of Earth's interior that lies between the crust and the outer core. Along with crust, the upper mantle forms the plates of plate tectonics.

**marine** living in or pertaining to the ocean or sea

**mass extinction** an event during Earth history when many species of living things became extinct, or were killed off, due to drastic changes in their environment.

**metamorphic rock** any rock that was created by a chemical or structural change to rock that already existed, from variations in pressure, temperature, and other physical conditions

**mollusk** a water-living invertebrate with an undivided body encased in one or two shells, such as shellfish

**molten** liquefied by heat

**mudstone** a fine-grained sedimentary rock consisting of hardened mud; related to shale but not layered

**nautiloid** a cephalopod that resembled a squid in a long, cone-shaped shell. These mollusks were predators that developed during the Ordovician Period.

**ocean ridge** an underwater mountain system through which lava escapes, resulting in seafloor spreading

**orogeny** process by which mountains are built. It involves folding, faulting, and uplifting of Earth's crust.

**paleontology** the study of forms of life that existed in past geological periods, including the study of plant and animal fossils

**petrified wood** a fossil formed by the replacement of minerals, usually silica, into the original wood of a tree

**photosynthesis** process by which plants form their own food from carbon dioxide and water through the action of sunlight in a green chemical called chlorophyll. A by-product or waste product of this process is oxygen.

**phylum** (plural is **phyla**) a major group into which plants or animals are classified

**plankton** organisms, such as microscopic algae and protozoans, that passively float or drift within a body of water and feed many animals

**plate tectonics** the theory that Earth's crust and part of the mantle are broken into about a dozen large plates (and several small ones) within the lithosphere. These planes move against and interact with one another.

**polyp** a tube-shaped bryozoan or coral animal that secretes a hard shell. The shells of large colonies become cemented together as reefs.

**protozoan** any of various one-celled organisms that usually get nourishment by taking in food particles, rather than by producing food through photosynthesis

**radioactive isotope** variation of a chemical element that differs in the number of neutrons but not the number of protons. These atoms emit energy in the forms of particles or waves, called radioactivity.

**reef** a large mound or ridge of rock within a body of water made from the exoskeletons of organisms such as corals and sponges cemented together

**relative age** the age of rocks and geologic events as determined by their position in chronological sequence, without taking into account how many years ago the rock or event might have occurred

**sandstone** a sedimentary rock made up of sand and usually including quartz. It is cemented together by silica, calcium carbonate, iron oxide, or clay.

**schist** a metamorphic rock derived from fine-grained sedimentary rock such as shale; forms in thin layers

**seafloor spreading** the process that forms new crust under the ocean. Earth's major tectonic plates are pushed apart by new volcanic rock formed when magma oozes out of the mantle from between the tectonic plates. As the lava hardens, continents riding on these plates are pushed apart.

**sediment** loose, uncemented pieces of rock or minerals carried and deposited by water, air, or ice. Sediment may include eroded sand, dirt particles, debris from living things, and solid materials that form as a result of chemical processes.

**sedimentary rock** rock composed of sediment, such as sandstone and limestone. Sedimentary rocks typically form beds, or layers.

**shale** finely layered sedimentary rock derived from mud formed by the hardening of clay, mud, or silt. When it is not layered, it is known as mudstone. About 70% of Earth's sedimentary rock is shale.

**silica** silicon dioxide ($SiO_2$) compounds that often take a crystalline form, especially quartz. Almost 60% of Earth's crust is composed of silica.

**species** the smallest category of plant or animal. One or more species are included in a genus. Members of a species tend to interbreed only with each other.

**subduction** the process by which oceanic crust moves down into the asthenosphere beneath a continental plate; occurs at trenches, called subduction zones

**supercontinent** giant landmass formed during Earth history and made up of several present-day continents. For example, the supercontinent Gondwana contained South America, Africa, southern Europe, the peninsula of India, Australia, and Antarctica.

**tectonic plate** any of a number of sections of Earth's lithosphere that floats on the asthenosphere and moves independently, sometimes rubbing against each other. The North American plate carries both the continent and part of the Atlantic Ocean.

**terrane** a fragment of crust that is bounded on all sides by faults and which has a geologic history different from adjacent blocks

**trace fossil** an impression or outline of an animal preserved in rock, such as a footprint

**trilobite** a crablike shelled marine animal (or close relative) present throughout the Paleozoic Era. These arthropods, now extinct, had a flattened, oval body in three vertical segments.

**unconformity** a surface of deposition in which the rock above is significantly younger than the rock below

**uplift** process in which a portion of the earth's crust is raised as a result of heat within the mantle. The crust can also be raised in response to tectonic forces, or large-scale movements deep within Earth.

**vascular** having or pertaining to veins, tubes through which fluid moves

**vertebrate** an animal with a backbone or spinal column; not an invertebrate

# FURTHER INFORMATION

## ONLINE WEB SITES

**Museum of Paleontology**
University of California at Berkeley
1101 Valley Life Sciences Building
Berkeley, CA 94720
www.ucmp.berkeley.edu/exhibit/exhibits.html
takes you through major exhibits in geology,
evolution, and the classification of living things
Also produced by UCMP is:
www.paleoportal.org
provides a link to many sites for anyone
interested in paleontology

**United States Geological Survey**
USGS National Center
12201 Sunrise Valley Drive
Reston, VA 20192
www.usgs.gov/education
The Learning Web introduces numerous topics and
projects related to earth science
Find out what's happening at Mount St. Helens
volcano: http://volcanoes.usgs.gov/
or where the earthquakes are:
http://earthquake.usgs.gov/

**The British Broadcasting Corporation** has major coverage of prehistoric life:
http://www.bbc.co.uk

## MUSEUMS

Be sure to look for museum web sites. Also, check university and public
museums in your area; they often have good geology exhibits.

### UNITED STATES
**American Museum of Natural History**
Central Park West at 79th St.
New York, NY 10024
www.amny.org

**Colorado School of Mines Geology Museum**
13th and Maple St.
Golden, CO 80401

**The Field Museum**
1400 S. Lake Shore Drive
Chicago, IL 60605
www.fieldmuseum.org
Look for the online exhibit about Sue, the best
preserved *Tyrannosaurus rex*

**University of Michigan Museum of Paleontology**
1109 Geddes Ave.,
Ann Arbor, MI 48109
www.paleontology.lsa.umich.edu

**Smithsonian National Museum of Natural History**
10th St. and Constitution Ave.
Washington, D.C. 20560
www.mnh.si.edu

### CANADA
**Geological Survey of Canada**
Earth Sciences Sector
601 Booth St.
Ottawa, Ontario K1A 0E8, Canada
http://ess.nrcan.gc.ca

**Canadian Museum of Nature**
240 McLeod St.
Ottawa, Ontario, K1P 6P4, Canada
www.nature.ca

**Provincial Museum of Alberta**
12845 102nd Ave.
Edmonton, Alberta T5N 0M6, Canada
www.prma.edmonton.ab.ca

**Manitoba Museum of Man and Nature**
190 Rupert Avenue
Winnipeg, Manitoba R3B 0N2, Canada
www.manitobamuseum.mb.ca

**Pacific Museum of the Earth**
6339 Stores Road
Vancouver, British Columbia V6T 1Z4, Canada
www.eos.ubc.ca

## DVDs

*Amazing Earth*, Artisan Entertainment, 2001

*Forces of Nature*—Book and DVD, National Geographic, 2004

*Living Rock: An Introduction to Earth's Geology,* WEA Corp, 2002
Also includes 400 USGS "Fact Sheets" in Adobe Acrobat format, obtainable on computer sytems with a
   DVD-ROM Drive)

*Physical Geography: Geologic Time,* TMW/Media Group, 2004

*Volcano: Nature's Inferno!,* National Geographic, 1997

## BOOKS

Anderson, Peter. *A Grand Canyon Journey: Tracing Time in Stone.* A First Book. Danbury, CT:
   Franklin Watts, 1997.

Ball, Jacqueline. *Earth's History.* Discovery Channel School Science series. Milwaukee, WI: Gareth
   Stevens Publishing, 2004.

Bonner, Hannah. *When Bugs Were Big : Prehistoric Life in a World Before Dinosaurs.* Washington, DC:
   National Geographic, 2004.

Castelfranchi, Yuri, and Nico Petrilli. *History of the Earth: Geology, Ecology, and Biology.* Hauppage,
   NY: Barrons, 2003.

Colson, Mary. *Earth Erupts.* Turbulent Earth series. Chicago: Raintree, 2005.

Colson, Mary. *Shaky Ground.* Turbulent Earth series. Chicago: Raintree, 2005.

Day, Trevor. *DK Guide to Savage Earth: An Earth Shattering Journey of Discovery.* New York: Dorling
   Kindersley, 2001.

Farndon, John. *How the Earth Works.* Pleasantville, NY: Reader's Digest, 1992.

Hooper, Meredith. *The Pebble in My Pocket: A History of Our Earth.* New York: Viking Books, 1996.

Lambert, David. *The Kingfisher Young People's Book of the Universe.* Boston: Kingfisher, 2001.

Maslin, Mark. *Earthquakes.* Restless Planet series. Chicago: Raintree, 2000.

Maynard, Christopher. *My Book of the Prehistoric World.* Boston: Kingfisher, 2001.

Oxlade, Chris. *The Earth and Beyond.* Chicago: Heinemann Library, 1999.

# INDEX